Chill
&
Unwind
COLORING
BOOK

Chill & Unwind
COLORING BOOK

PEACEFUL IMAGES TO SPARK YOUR IMAGINATION

ANDREA SARGENT

THUNDER BAY
P·R·E·S·S
San Diego, California

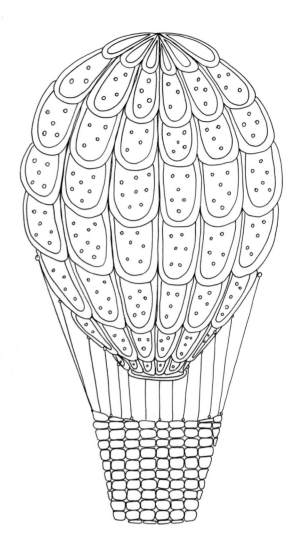

Thunder Bay Press
An imprint of Printers Row Publishing Group
10350 Barnes Canyon Road, Suite 100, San Diego, CA 92121
www.thunderbaybooks.com

Text and design © 2019 Arcturus Holdings Limited
Illustrations © Andrea Sargent

Printers Row Publishing Group is a division of Readerlink Distribution Services, LLC.
Thunder Bay Press is a registered trademark of Readerlink Distribution Services, LLC.

All notations of errors or omissions should be addressed to Thunder Bay Press, Editorial Department, at the above address. All other correspondence (author inquiries, permissions) concerning the content of this book should be addressed to Arcturus Holdings Limited, 26/27 Bickels Yard, 151-153 Bermondsey Street, London SE1 3HA, info@arcturuspublishing.com

Thunder Bay Press
Publisher: Peter Norton
Associate Publisher: Ana Parker
Publishing/Editorial Team: April Farr, Kelly Larsen, Kathryn C. Dalby
Editorial Team: JoAnn Padgett, Melinda Allman, Dan Mansfield

ISBN: 978-1-68412-939-3
CH007371NT

Printed in China
23 22 21 20 19   2 3 4 5 6

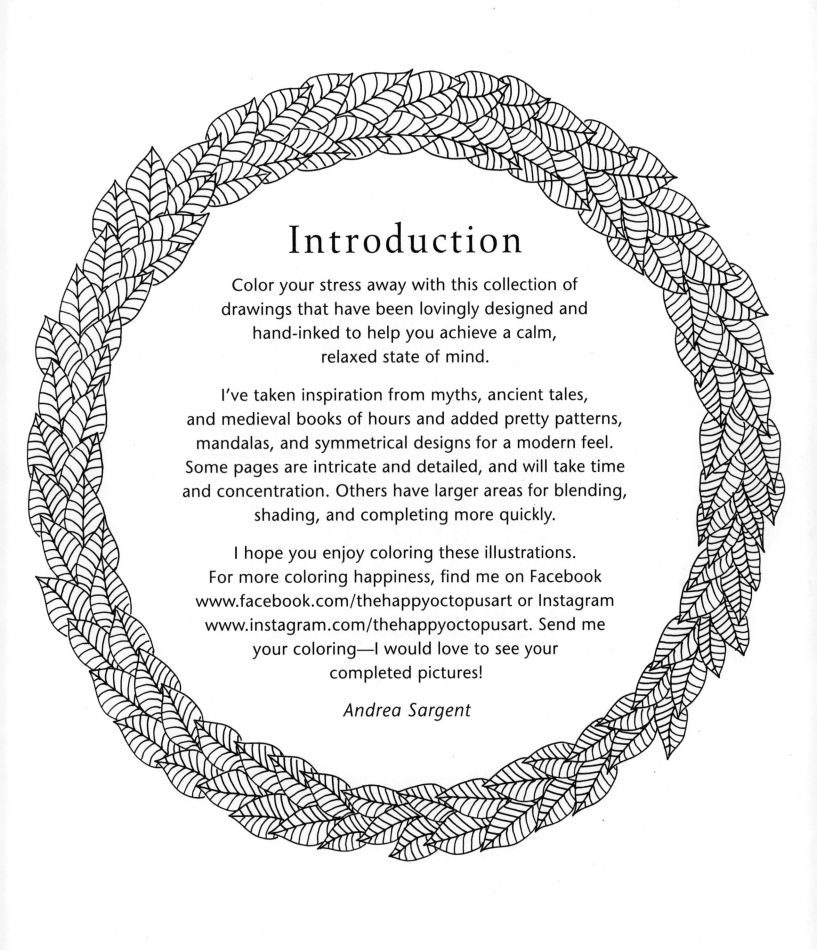

Introduction

Color your stress away with this collection of
drawings that have been lovingly designed and
hand-inked to help you achieve a calm,
relaxed state of mind.

I've taken inspiration from myths, ancient tales,
and medieval books of hours and added pretty patterns,
mandalas, and symmetrical designs for a modern feel.
Some pages are intricate and detailed, and will take time
and concentration. Others have larger areas for blending,
shading, and completing more quickly.

I hope you enjoy coloring these illustrations.
For more coloring happiness, find me on Facebook
www.facebook.com/thehappyoctopusart or Instagram
www.instagram.com/thehappyoctopusart. Send me
your coloring—I would love to see your
completed pictures!

Andrea Sargent

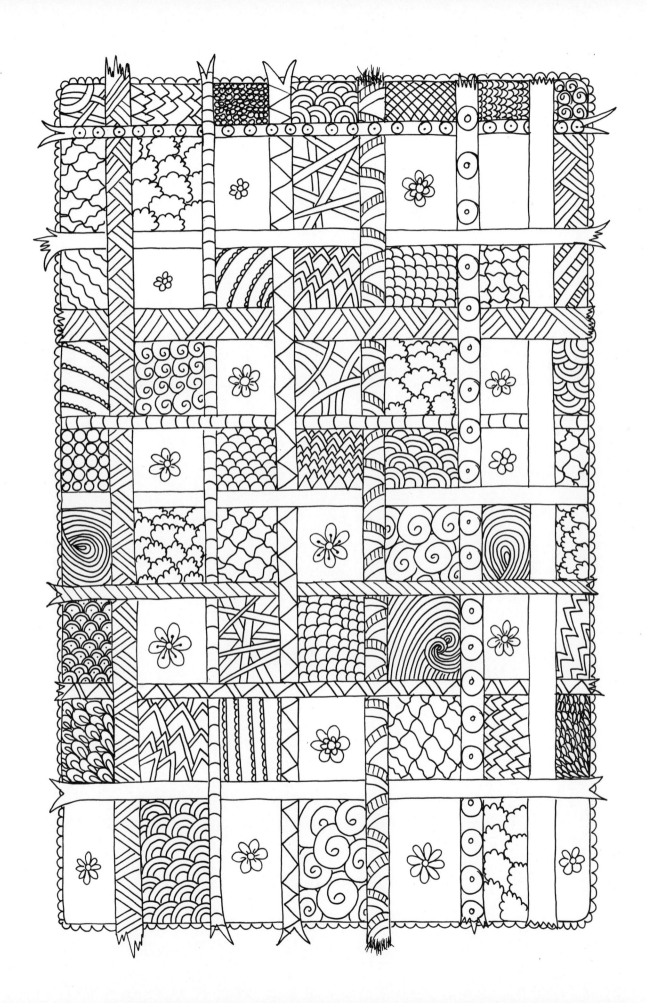

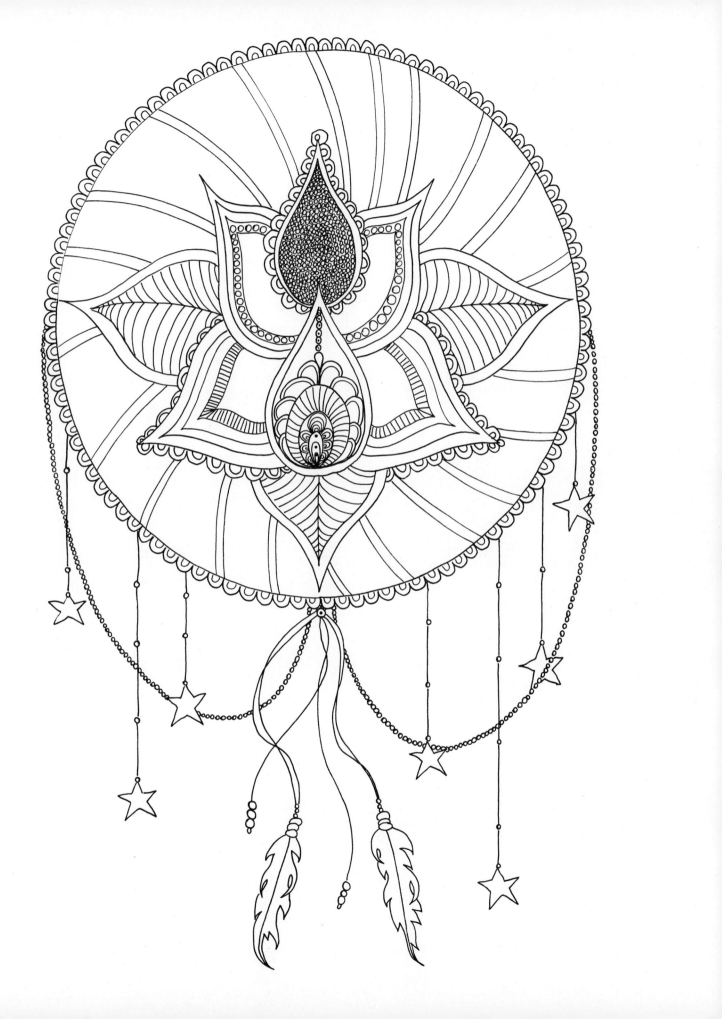

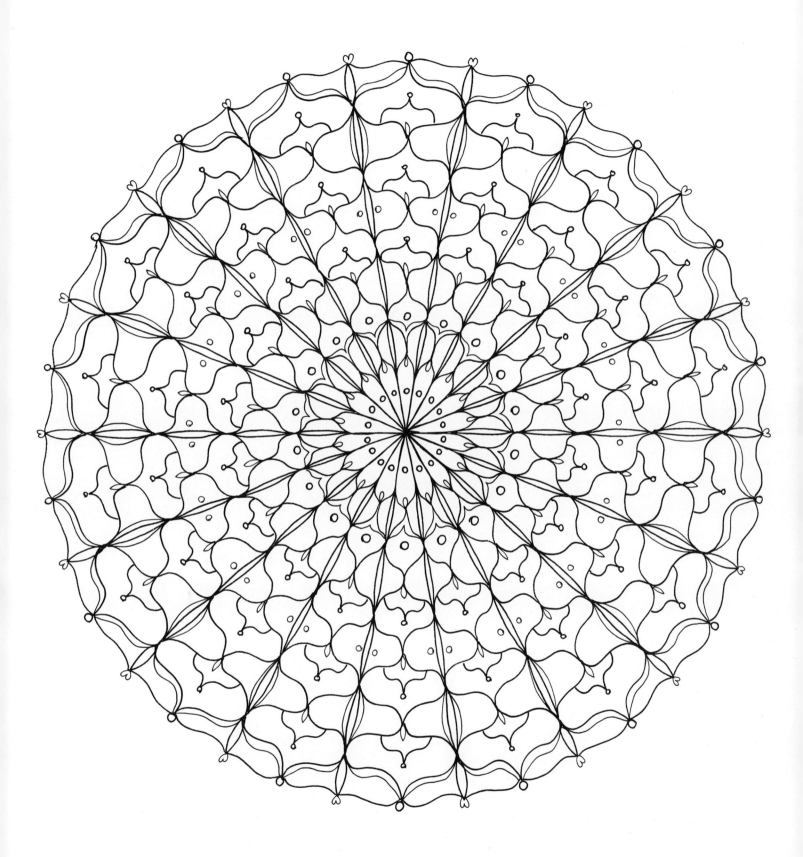

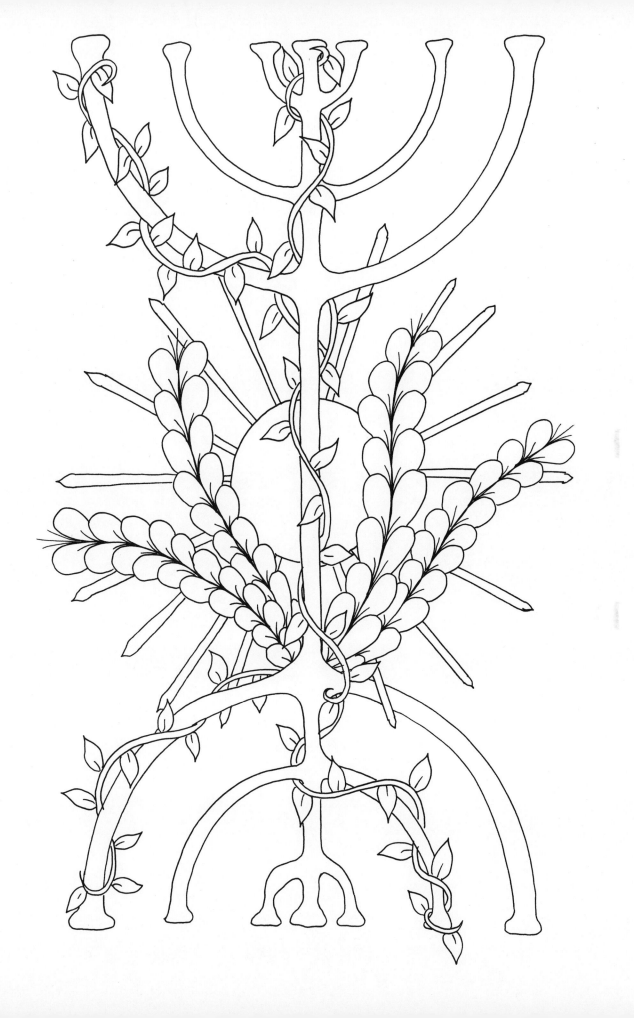

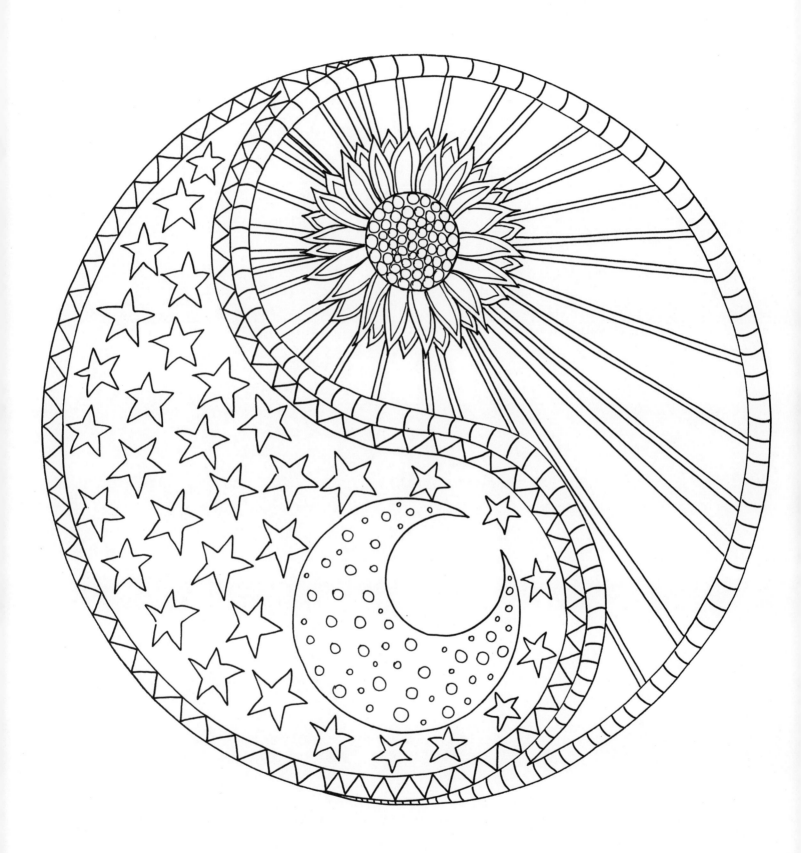

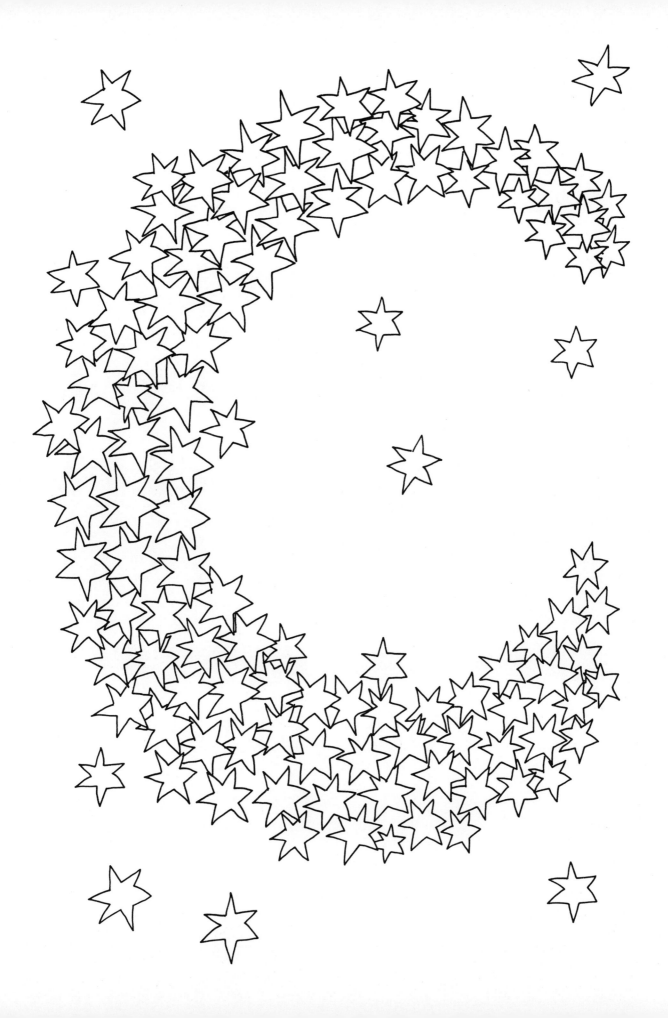

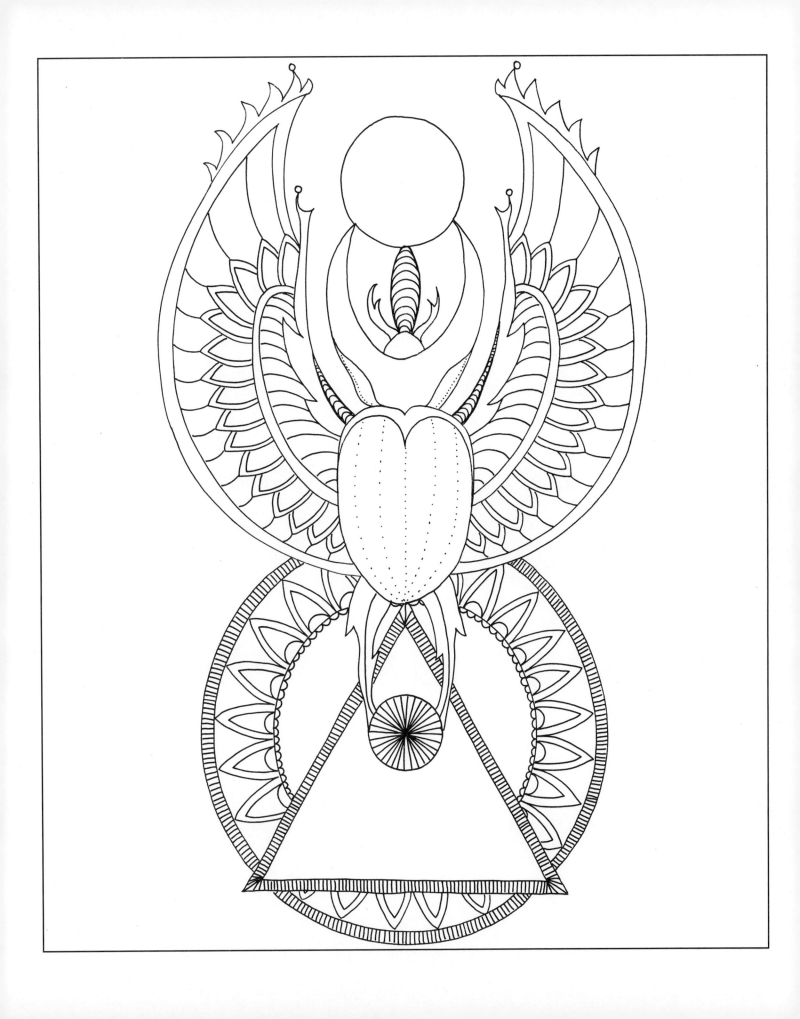

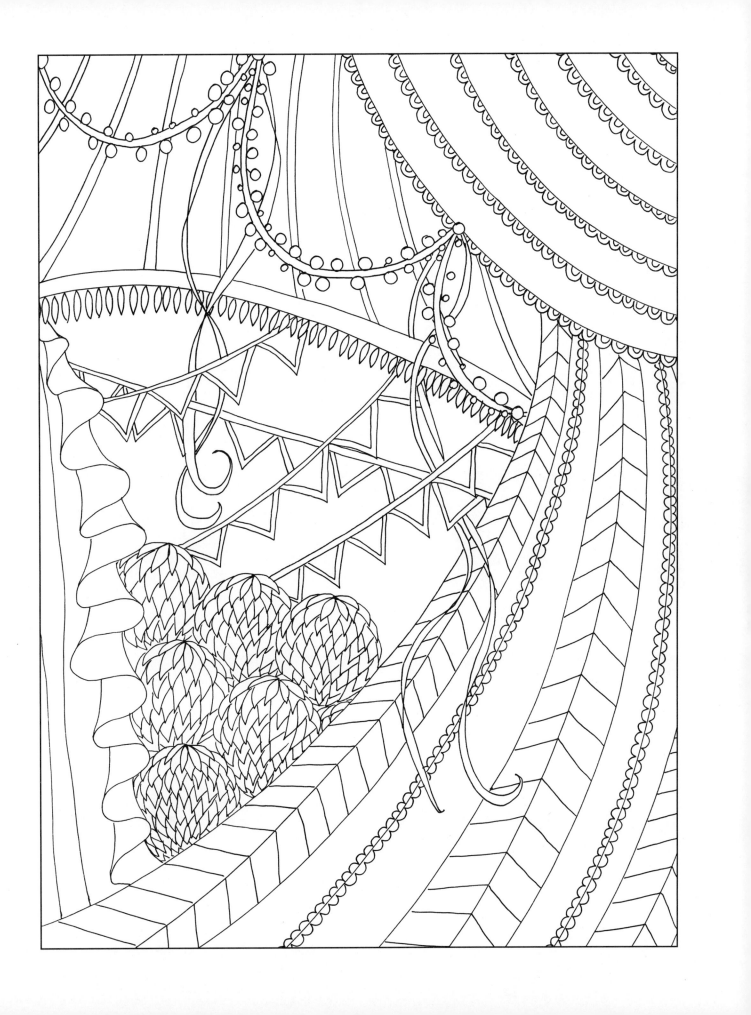

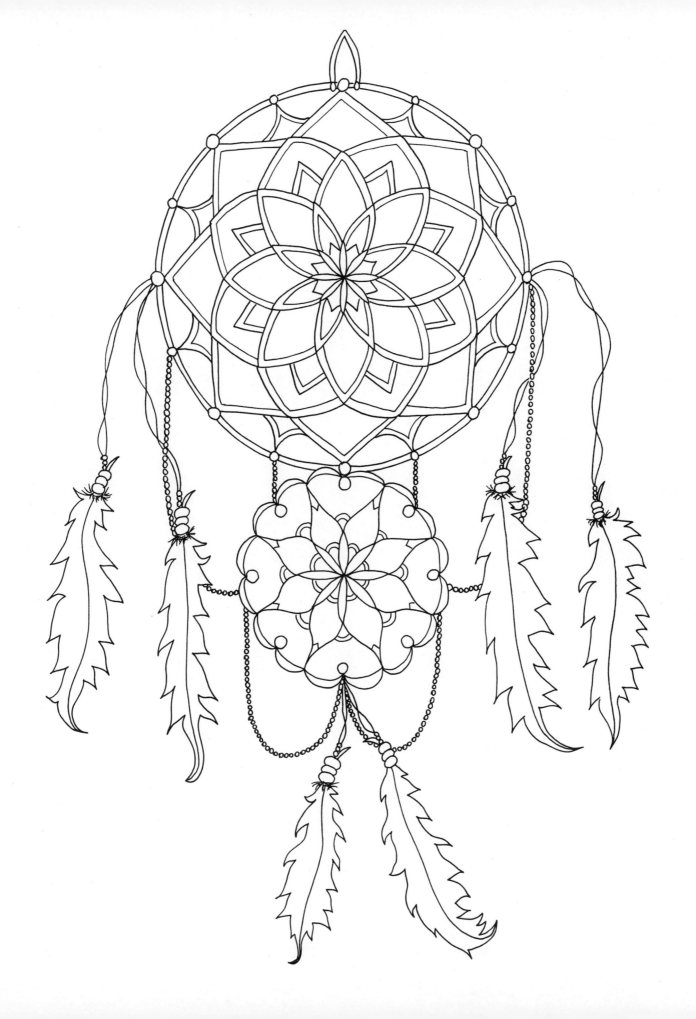

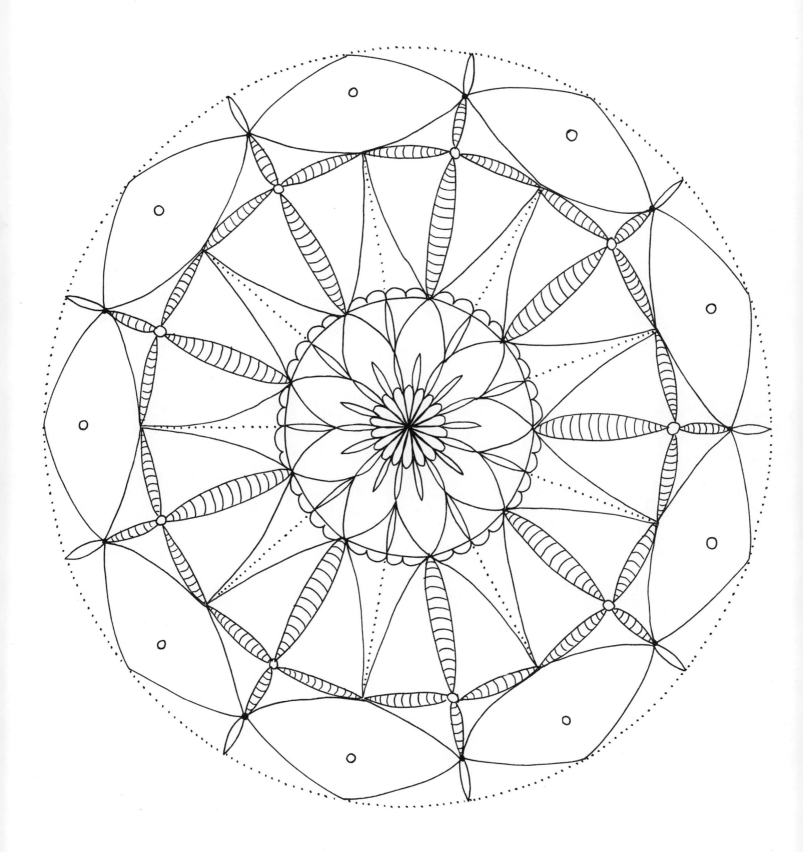

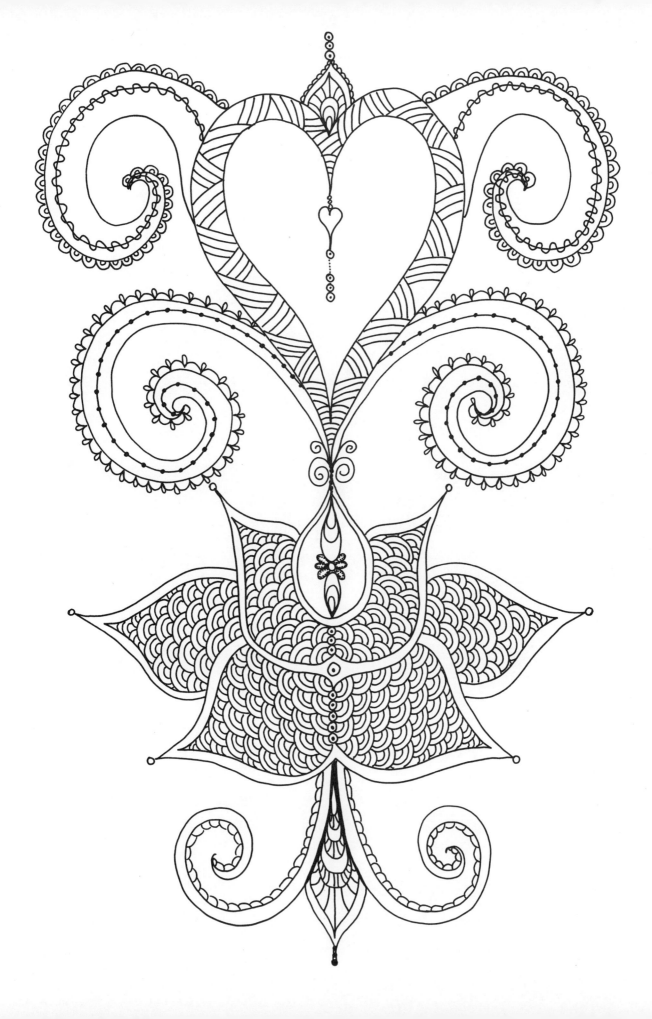